BLACK,
BLIND,
AND
FEMALE

BLACK, BLIND, AND FEMALE

Inspiration to Overcome Obstacles

Kari Kelley

authorHOUSE®

AuthorHouse™ LLC
1663 Liberty Drive
Bloomington, IN 47403
www.authorhouse.com
Phone: 1-800-839-8640

Published by AuthorHouse 04/09/2014

ISBN: 978-1-4685-6339-9 (sc)
ISBN: 978-1-4685-6861-5 (e)

Library of Congress Control Number: 2012905265

Foreword

It is my belief that each of us is born for a purpose, and Kari is a prime example of a woman who is actively pursuing her purpose.

I've known Kari since she was five (5) and she has shown her passion for reaching out to others i.e., seemingly always wanting to see others happy or perform plain old fashion problem solving. Her contagious laughter and sense of humor has a way of lifting you from whatever is negatively affecting you.

Kari has been faced with, seemingly, insurmountable challenges but due to her tenacity she has forged ahead and overcome. She seems to bear up under difficulties with confidence and she gives God the credit.

I am very proud of my goddaughter, Kari. And without reservation, her book will touch the heart of all who read her life's highway.

Alice Arnold
Godmother

Introduction

While the title states the outward demographic the story is about what cannot be seen by the naked eyes. Adopted, abused and determined grace the inner core and tell a story of alchemy. Kari's life began with a series of events and circumstances that make her feel that her life is not worth much more than throw away base metal. However, over the course of time that base metal serves as the foundation for priceless golden wisdom. Through resources, unseen helpers, and a deep determination Kari uses her experiences to bring awareness to topics that are controversial and uncomfortable in an effort to stop abuse and provide an example of what is possible to overcome.

PART ONE
1973-1983

"I'm Three!"

I remember sitting on Santa's lap. I told him what I wanted for Christmas and he said if I was a good girl I would get it. Also I remember a grown up telling me on my birthday that I was four years old. Having been taught to say that I was three years old, I kept telling everyone that I was three. So in complete confidence I put my four year old hands on my four year old hip and stamped my little four year old foot and said in no uncertain terms that, "I am three!"

One day I was eating Muncho's potato chips at the kitchen table and I dropped one on the floor. The nice foster lady slipped on it, fell and started to cry. She stayed in bed for a long time. After that, another grown up came and told me that I was going to have a new "mommy" and "daddy" and that I was going to live with them. When my new mommy and daddy came to take me with them, I didn't want to go. But, the grownups said that I was going to a new house and that I would be happy. Little did anyone know how unhappy I would be. Sobbing as all of my things were loaded into their car, I was still crying as I climbed into the back seat. Frances, my new mommy turned around and said, "Shut up all that noise!" This is the beginning of many silent tears I would cry.

New Home, New Me

What I remember next was going to many different houses and meeting a lot of grownups who were called auntie and uncle and cousin. At my new house, I walked into my very own bedroom which was right next to my parents' room. Now I was happy. I thought I was so special to have my own bedroom. No one else who lived in my new house had their own bedroom. I was the only girl. I felt like my room was such a beautiful place. In my mind's eye I can still see the door closed and Frances standing behind me telling me to open the door. I did and I walked into a pink and white paradise. Right in the middle of the room stood this beautiful pink and white canopy bed. There were dolls with pretty dresses on shelves and pretty curtains on the windows. I loved it.

Gradually my room stopped being my beautiful paradise. First, I broke the dolls. They were all porcelain and they were only for show. I didn't know that I was not supposed to play with them. Then, I remember how angry Frances got. She yelled at me. "How could you be so stupid? \Didn't you know how much money those dolls were worth? This room was a showplace. People used to pay to come and look at this room and you just tore this room up"

Next, I broke the bed by trying to swing on the wooden frame across the top. The frame looked like the bars at school that I could jump up and swing on. First, Frances gave me a beating with the broken piece and then she replaced my bed. The new bed was hard and it had drawers underneath and it didn't match the rest of the furniture.

In spite of the changes, my bedroom was still my favorite place to be, my refuge from the world, until I had to share it with real living, breathing, walking and talking monsters. One of which was a neice that lived in Oakland California. Her name was Brandy. She was slightly older than me and I believe she was jelous because she had been the only girl until I was adopted. She came to live with us during the summer and during the holidays. During the first Christmas with my new family, she came and I remember getting a doll and a teddy bear. I loved them both and she made them disappear before the day was done. This would prove to be the least of the cruelty she would inflict on me. Brandy was skilled at getting Frances to believe that my black eye or busted lip was a result of my clumsiness. I remember telling the truth about what really happened and I learned quickly how creative Brandy could be. I spent entire nights on my bedroom floor with no blankets. Bubble gum found it's way mysteriously into my hair. As we got older her cruelty reached new hights

As I began to adapt to my new home and family, I started to realize things about myself that I didn't know before. I learned to cover my mouth when I smiled or laughed because I had "rabbit teeth." Then I learned that my skin color was not quite light enough and it wasn't quite dark enough either, so I often was described as being "piss colored" by my new family and their friends. Next, I found out that since it was not so easy to run a comb through my hair, I was "nappy headed." In the beginning, Frances straightened my hair with an iron comb that you can heat up on the stove. Every Sunday morning I would have a lump in my throat and my stomach twisted into knots when I heard the kitchen drawer open. Then the clakety-clak of the straightening comb and hot curling rod being placed on the stove and the clicking of the gas burner coming on. I dreaded what came next. I had to sit on a chair close to the stove and I sat there crying silently.

After a while Frances paid other people to deal with my hair. I spent whole Saturdays in a beauty shop with relaxer burning my scalp because my hair was so coarse that it took a long time to straighten. I sat under a dryer for what felt like weeks because my hair was so thick it took a long time to dry. Sometimes I got my hair corn rowed. Other times I wore a wig when no one had the time or money to deal with my hair. Kids had lots of fun pulling it off and running away with it.

Another imperfection was that my eyes were not like everyone else's. I was called "cross eyed" (pronounced cross-sided); what I came to understand as I got older was that I was visually impaired or legally blind. Frances did what she could by taking me to one doctor after another trying to "get my eyes fixed." I wore glasses and I had special devices to use in order to see things more clearly, all of which were either lost or broken soon after I acquired them. These devices helped somewhat but since the damage is to the optic nerves, nothing short of a medical breakthrough would restore my vision.

Eventually I learned how to act like I could see more than I really could. I didn't need perfect eyesight to see that I was one ugly girl. I also had plenty of people around me to remind me including Frances.

About the time I turned five, I began to be introduced to ways that I could be pretty and loved.

Survival Skills

Skillful hands touched me, arms wrapped me in warm hugs. Those hands fisted in my nappy hair and guided my mouth between their legs. It was one thing when the hands belonged to the guys. I wanted so desperately to be loved so I make sure I did exactly what I was told. I became an expert by the age of seven. Then that summer Brandy came to stay and decided if I could do it for the boys that I could do it for her. She had a totally different teaching method. Brandy knew that the person that I was most afraid of was Frances. Both Brandy and I also knew that Frances would believe anything Brandy said about me, so along with beatings and threats to expose me to Frances she also got me to use my oral skills to keep her satisfied.

There was an awkward balance to how I dealt with the confusion of my life. When I initiated what I thought was innocent contact, I was rebuffed. Frances interpreted my actions as me being "fast" and "always trying to be up in some man's face." I finally figured out that I was only beautiful and perfect when I was the secret toy that could only be played with when no one else was looking.

Frances worked as an in home care giver and sometimes she took me to work with her where she took care of people in wheelchairs or people who were bedridden. There were times when she had two such jobs so I might sleep at one jobsite and go to a different one after school.

When I was eight years old she would drop me off at an aunt's home where I would stay. A school bus picked me up and dropped me off there before and after school. Then Frances picked me up after she got off work.

I was able to use my "special powers" to receive love and affection at my aunt's house as well. One particular day when Frances dropped me off I was so busy that I missed the school bus. I was persuaded to take things to a whole new level. This was the day that I was stripped naked and I felt pain like nothing that I had felt before. My mouth was covered as I screamed and cried and the blood was wiped off. Then I was told how much trouble I would be in if I told anyone. Later that day, when Frances picked me up, I was so scared that she knew I'd missed school, and that I had been "fast." I wet my pants in the car on the way home and got a whipping. Ironically enough she never found out that I missed school or that I had been raped that day.

Four years later when I was twelve, I was awakened by someone trying to get in my bed. I would tuck the covers under the mattress and try to get in the bed without them coming out. So my visitor had to lift the mattress to get into the bed.I woke up while he was there and we had this conversation about what he was doing and he was drunk. While we were talking, Frances woke up and heard things going on in my bedroom in the wee hours. While she didn't say a word that night,she did call other family members to discuss it.

"Off To School"

One place my "special powers" never came in handy was at school. Being "that piss colored, cross eyed, bucktooth, nappy headed (or wig wearing) girl," made going to school not so nice for me.

When I did bother to wear glasses, there was a slight improvement in my vision. Depending on what I needed to see, however, I had to take the glasses off sometimes or wear them in addition to using an additional device like a magnifying glass. I didn't necessarily wear the latest fashions either so I was definitely a target for getting picked on, teased and sometimes beaten up. More so in the public school system than in the private school that I would attend starting in 6th grade. One thing that I remember about public school was that some of the teachers made me an example that no other student wanted to live up to. For example if I got a perfect score on a test the teacher would say to the class, "This little girl who can't even see very well got a perfect score on her test. I think that is amazing."

My answer to that was to stop getting perfect scores and cut down on being so "amazing" at school. However, when the report cards came home and the parent/teacher conferences were attended I had to make choices about the worst of two evils; the beatings at school or what happened when Frances got me home away from those teachers.

Because of my vision disability there were also special instructors who would teach me how to do things like cross the street, take busses, and go shopping. These were not simple to do with limited vision. Before I was allowed to cross a real street I played with matchbox cars on a board with felt that represented streets and intersections. Taking busses involved making sure I asked the driver lots of questions and making sure they let me know when they reached my stop.

Going shopping in my early life meant learning the layout of the store, finding the candy aisle and scanning the shelves from left to right first and then up and down using whatever device was not lost or broken at the time.

I had numerous instructors as I attended school and some of them made huge differences in my life. As I look back I remember that there was one instructor who had shorter legs than me, so when we walked, I would walk really fast to make her run to keep up with me. She had a dog that was very friendly and she brought that dog to our lessons. I remember being so grossed out when she would let the dog lick her on the mouth.

One day I went with one of the instructors to pick her daughter up at a dance class and I watched in fascination and awe. After that, I harbored a secret dream to be a dancer. Frances told me, the day I came home from seeing the dance class, "I better not hear a tale of you trying to dance, shaking your tail and carrying on." Another one of these instructors paid the tuition for me to attend a private school from the sixth through the eighth grades

When I was ten Frances had a stroke that left her paralyzed on her right side. In spite of this setback, she still managed to do a lot from her wheelchair. She could still cook and she ran a candy store in our house for a while to bring in extra money. When the instructors came to my house to teach me how to cook and clean Frances was rude to them and mean to me. She would say, "I don't know why these white folks think I can't teach my child how to do things around this house." I eventually told them to stop coming. As a result, to this day I do not like to cook. If I don't have a step by step recipe, I will not attempt the dish. It's no surprise that my crockpot and my casserole dishes are my best friends in the kitchen. I can throw the ingredients in and go on about my business. Although I can clean house, there are certain techniques I could have learned that would have made it much easier and given me more confidence to get the cleaning done right. One thing was vacuuming in a grid pattern and dusting by putting spray cleaner on the rag or sponge instead of directly on the surface of what I needed to clean.

Frances was a very good cook and she was famous at church and during the holidays for her dressing and sweet potato pies. I don't have the skills nor the taste for most of what she cooked. I get teased sometimes for the fact that I don't like "Soul Food." I don't like my food touching on my plate, and if there is something that has juice or sauce, I want it on a separate plate or in a bowl, all by itself. For example, I put mashed potatoes and gravy in a bowl and on a separate plate I put meat and bread on yet another plate. Another will be for the salad or other vegetable.

Time for Church

I spent a great deal of time in church. Almost everyone in our house attended church. There were services on Friday nights that started at 7:30, and on Sundays the first service was Sunday school at 10 a.m. Regular church service was at 12 noon and ended around 2 p.m. There was a service for the youth that started at 6:30 p.m., and the last service of the day started at 8 p.m. and ended at about 10 p.m.

In the years before Frances' stroke, I remember everyone piling in the car, a green Chevy Impala, and Frances driving us to and from church. Once she was no longer able to drive, different family members drove the two of us until they moved away. Then, although he never went to church, Frances's husband dropped us off and picked us up.

It was in church that I found out I could sing. I was a member of the children's choir from around age seven. During this time, there was a radio station that played gospel music every Sunday, and I sang along with the radio. I knew all the songs that the adult choir sang because my relatives were in that choir and sometimes they took me to choir rehearsals with them. Frances had kept a tight hold on me when it came to dancing and singing anything that was not gospel. When she caught me singing a sitcom theme song, she told me to, "Shut up singing that devil's music."

For the most part Frances put on a good front for the folks at church. Most of the church members thought very highly of her.

But there were times that she let her mask slip. One day, when I was about nine years old, I was sitting in the choir stand and the pastor was preaching. I was whispering to my friend when Frances got up from her seat and walked to the choir stand, pointed her finger at me, and said, "Kari, you shut up your mouth!" Then she went back to her seat and sat down.

The pastor just said, "Amen," and kept right on preaching. Another incident took place when I was performing at church in the Christmas play. I had the role of the oldest daughter in the family. In the scene, my mother came in and told me to redo the dusting of the furniture because I hadn't done it right the first time. At that moment, Frances chose to tell the entire congregation that I was not good at cleaning at home either. I was mortified with embarrassment. This was a special program with visitors who came for the occasion. Frances had done that in front of everyone. In spite of my embarrassment, however, I continued and the play went on without further interruptions.

I never know if anyone talked to her about this behavior and at the time I thought no one cared about me feelings anyway. Frances told me on more than one occasion that she had done me a favor by adopting me since I was "half blind and ugly" and no one else would have. I concluded that since I was not the "flesh and blood" of my adopted family, everyone ignored any mistreatment I received.

Almost Like Family

Once Frances had the stroke she began to be hospitalized frequently. Whenever she went into the hospital I would stay with my cousins. Altogether there were six kids. For the most part I liked being with my cousins. I always knew that I would be going home when Frances came home from the hospital. It never occurred to me that I would end up living there for good. I was staying with them when Frances passed away in 1983. It was one thing for me to be there temporarily but once I realized that I was now going to have to live with five kids who were blood related I immediately felt like "the outsider." Since I was the outsider, it was very hard for me to adjust. First I had to get used to sharing a bedroom and doing chores in turn. Next there were rules that I had to get used to. Rule number one: make the bed before you leave the house, and don't leave without eating breakfast. I managed these things okay but now I'm thirteen years old, living in a new house and I start wetting the bed. This would happen sporadically for awhile. The news of my bed wetting along with any other information that could be talked about made its way to church and then to school. There was one boy who went to the same church and the same school as me. So, anything that happened at my new home got talked about at church and then made its way to school and vice versa. Needless to say I spent more time being embarrassed and teased.

I remember thinking about the people who were good to me and wondering why I didn't end up living with them. Frances had a married son who had four kids. He was the "cool dad." His two middle sons had birthdays close to mine and he would buy a big cake and we would have a combined birthday party. Even though he was older he still treated me like I was his little sister. He would sing a song for me and grab my nose. Anywhere his kids went I went too. He never thought it was strange for me to play with army men and marbles and climb trees instead of playing with dolls.

I had a nephew who called me Toots and told me funny stories about "the little man that lived in my chin." He and his girlfriend would take me skating and shopping and just let me hang out with them especially during Thanksgiving and Christmas. They would eat at our house and then go to her house and after that to his mom's house and any of their friends and other family members. There would be a bunch of food from all these different places.

They always bought me cool Christmas presents like one year they got me a record player with a projector and I pretended I had my own movie theater.

I had another cousin who was in college and who lived with us. He and his fiancé would take me to school with them. I remember having to sit on her lap everywhere we went because his car was a two-seater. I remember they took me to Malibu Grand Prix once and I got to drive a car around the track. I crashed a lot. I was in their wedding and I tore my dress at the reception. I remember when they brought their first baby over to see us. I got to hold her and I thought she was so cute until she spit up on me.

I even gave serious thought to living with Mr. H's (France's husband) mistress. She had a granddaughter who was the same age as me so I spent a lot of time over there. Whenever she had parties I went and I met other kids from her school and I went fun places with that family. In reality there may have been a possibility of this if certain circumstances had been different.

My parents' marriage was not a happy one. Frances said she was married to a pair of pants in the closet because the pants spent more time at home than he did. He didn't change all that much once she had the stroke. Maybe four out of seven days he came home from work and ate dinner in front of the television, showered, changed clothes, and left the house until about ten or eleven at night. I remember times when the phone would ring and if anyone besides him answered, the person would hang up. Eventually even I could tell when he was on the phone with his mistress because he would talk low and quiet. One day Frances picked up the phone and listened in on the conversation. When they told each other, "I love you," Frances said, "I'm glad to know y'all love each other." The man ran into the living room and everything got loud and violent.

On many occasions there were loud arguments about divorce, but it never happened. I can't even imagine what my life would have been like if they had gotten a divorce. Since neither one of them actually loved me,

I imagined their battles would have been more along the lines of them fighting about who would get stuck with me. I had nightmares about them saying things like, "What the hell am I gonna do with her? You're the one that wanted to adopt her."

Frances would say, "I know that but I don't want her either."

I spent countless hours fantasizing about what my life would have been like if I had perfect vision or long beautiful hair. I made up stories in my head out what my birth family was like. I decided they were hidden royalty and I had to be separated in order for me to be safe from people who wanted to kill the heir to a royal throne. Those were the good days. I probably spent more time hating my birth family for not wanting me. One thing I didn't do was desire to find out who they were.

PART TWO
1984-1994

Life After Frances

I started the eighth grade the September after Frances died. I had gone to the same school for the sixth and seventh grades, so I didn't have to change schools even though I had moved. The school was small and it only went up to the eighth grade. One bright spot at this time was becoming a cheerleader for the school basketball team.

For me, being a cheerleader was the closest I would ever get to making that dream of being a dancer come true. I loved being a cheerleader; even though, I was horrible at it, I did it. I have bad hand—eye coordination, and at the time, I was very skinny. I was not graceful at all. I think people probably came to the games just to get a good laugh from watching me. But, anytime I was in my cheerleader uniform and the team was winning, I could avoid the misery of not having any friends. I was one of the team.

Just before I graduated from the eighth grade I was able to perform in a school talent show, so my classmates got to hear me sing. I'll never forget overhearing one of the students saying, "At least she can do something."

Here Comes High School

During my high school years, one thing that kept me distracted was moving back and forth between the house I grew up in and my cousins' house. No matter which house I was in, I always wanted to be in the other one. When I was with my cousins I had to deal with five siblings who were related to each other by blood. I always felt like an outsider there. So, I would make a fuss and end up back in the house with France's husband, my adoptive dad.

Living with him was definitely not the best place for me but because, he worked all day, and no one else lived there, it was easy for me to cut school. Anytime I got to be alone, I could escape the misery of feeling like an outsider.

My craving for love and attention stayed with me through high school and once my body changed and I grew to a height of five feet ten, most of it legs, I discovered extensions and acrylic nails and I had to make sure they stayed maintained. My hair hung to my waist in long, thin single braids. Some of the people who I went to school with in the eighth grade went on to the same high school as I did so I was still "that cross eyed girl," and I still had buck teeth. In school I remained the "broken doll no one wanted to be seen playing with." Somehow one person managed to begin to have feelings for me. I'm not surehow it happened but for me it was nice to be loved. This was a relationship that had to be kept a secret because it was not acceptable for two girls to be together. This relationship lasted for a while but eventually I had to realize that I was in it because I was starving for anything that felt like love and it didn't matter where or who it came from.

Between all the moving and cutting school and sneaking around I fell behind. In the summer of 1987, I was living with Mr. H. and on Father's Day weekend he found out that I was not going to graduate on time. First, he went into his customary shouting, interrogating mode. He yelled questions that he never gave me time to answer. Then he'd go and do something like watch TV or fix some food, and then come back and yell at me some more. Next, he took me to an area of the neighborhood where the drunks, prostitutes, and drug addicts hung out. He then proceeded to tell me that I was not even good enough to end up like one of them because I would never amount to anything.

I decided that he was right, and that I was better off dead. I was afraid to cut my wrists and we didn't have drugs or alcohol in the house, so I poured insect repellant into a soda and drank it. At the time I didn't know it wouldn't kill me; all I knew was I just wanted the misery that was my life to end. He took me to the hospital telling me how he wished I was a boy so he could just kick my ass and throw me out. What I didn't say out loud was that being a girl was not always a problem for him.

So I did my seventy two hours in Stanford's Children's Psych ward with kids who had eating disorders, terminal illness, or who, like me, had attempted suicide. I carefully skirted the delicate questions about what happened to make me want to end my life. I was convinced that now that I was seventeen the only place I would end up if Social Services got involved was some group home or worse. I focused everything on my problems in school. One of the requirements during my stay was to have a counseling session with Mr. H. Mr. H was his belligerent self and the session went in circles. I went back home with Mr. H after my time was up. One night after a shouting match I stood over him with a butcher's knife in my hand while he, oblivious, slept. What stopped me from cutting his throat was knowing I would have to go to jail. If *CSI* or *Law and Order* had been around in 1987 I might not be the free woman that I am today.

I started what should have been my senior year living with Mr. H and made plans to go back to that high school and get a diploma rather than take a GED.

About that time, Mr. H met a very nice lady and got married. He sold the house I had grown up in and moved in with her. I went with him but yet again I was this outsider and I started moving again. I finally settled at my brother Lonnie's house.

I actually did manage to graduate, class of 1989. I tried to go to community college but I didn't stay with it. I decided that I should just find a full time job and try and make it on my own.

Kari Goes to Work

I had a few part time jobs during high school and I worked as a receptionist in the high school's main office. While I did that, I decided that being a receptionist was easy enough for me to do and I didn't need to get some fancy degree just to answer phones. So I found a job working as a CBX operator for the Palo Alto Clinic on evenings and weekends.

In June 1991, I got my first full time job working as a front desk reception for Telesensory. I was not professional at all. In fact, I was the walking advertisement for "How to be Unprofessional and Look Like a Tramp." Every outfit I wore had to be short, tight, or both. I kept my hair and my nails done. I swore constantly, made personal calls, and carried out my clerical duties inconsistently. In spite of all that I held that job for eight years. It was on that job that I met my soul mate and fell in love.

A Man? For Me? Really?

I did have a few relationships during high school but they all ended badly. The male attention I received on my jobs and as I walked to and from bus stops gave me a feeling of being beautiful, which I had been craving all my life.

The first time I saw him I thought he was the finest man on two legs. Willie Kelley was a tall milk chocolate colored man with an *S Curl* in his hair. He had broad shoulders and muscular arms, and his smile lit up my world. All of which happened before he ever said a word to me.

I'd seen Willie at a "catering truck" getting some food, but since there were a few other businesses in the area so I didn't realize he worked at my place. When he casually strolled through the lobby and said hello, I almost fell off my chair. Later that week I was properly introduced.

In October 1990, I was able to get my very first apartment. After overhearing me discuss having a house-warming party, Willie tried to get an invitation. However, after thinking more about it, I decided against throwing the party. I was way too embarrassed to have people see my mismatched, raggedy furniture and besides, I already shared my place with some house guests, roaches.

But, Willie invited me out to celebrate my new place. It would be a dual celebration as Willie turned forty that same month. I took the entire week to find the perfect outfit and finally settled on a very short, pour me into, white stretch dress, a short sleeved matching jacket and hot pink high heels with the matching bag. When I was finished getting dressed, I paced around and kept second guessing everything. Willie showed up at my door with a single rose in his hand. I had to borrow a vase from my neighbor.

Most guys I had dealt with before didn't come to the door. They sat outside and blew the car horn (if they had a car that is). I would come out and they would lean over to let me in the car.

Willie was a breath of fresh air. He opened my car door. He opened the door to the restaurant and pulled out my chair. Before this, I was used to a drive through or a place that had booths or somebody just showing up with some fast food that to eat in the car.

Needless to say, I was on cloud nine and also a nervous wreck. On our way home, he asked if I would like to spend the night with him; of course, I said yes. Our first date, October 20, 1990, was the day I fell in love. He took me to his house and gave me a magical night. He had a fireplace in his bedroom. He lit candles and put on some soft music. And, he made me a drink in an actual brandy snifter. Never mind that I was only twenty at the time.

This man, the man of my dreams, actually had a house. Now that was amazing. I was used to guys renting motel rooms or trying to do the deed before someone came home (like his mom for example). Since I just got my place, I wasn't prepared to have overnight guests. I neither had brandy snifters nor candles, and it had never crossed my mind to buy things like that. All I had were some plastic plates and cups.

Willie had the kind of stuff that I only ever saw in movies or read about in books.

We had breakfast in the morning and he took me home. What a come down from his place to my roach infested one bedroom apartment.

That Monday I couldn't wait to see him at work. Willie, on the other hand, was cool as a cucumber. I wanted a committed relationship, but he was just enjoying a casual thing with a twenty year old. Willie had been married and lost his wife to lung cancer in 1987. Also, he had been in a relationship that ended about six months before we met. Now we also had to work together and it was hard to realize that I wouldn't be with him anymore. It was absolute misery for me. I felt rejected and hurt.

Finally, I decided to move on, and I met another man, who was very affectionate, which made me feel good. He was so romantic. He would show up with flowers for no special occasion, and he wrote love song lyrics on cards and left them in strategic places for me to find. However, I learned that all that glitters ain't necessarily gold.

After he moved in with me, he confessed that his checks were being garnished for back child support, and he couldn't pay his share of the expenses. He also had a habit of telling me that he would be home at a certain time and not showing up until hours later.

I decided that it was time for me to move. I found a tiny studio that was not going to be large enough for both of us. I gave my notice to both my landlord and my boyfriend. The break up was not a clean one. I didn't like being without a man, so I would go back into the relationship, and we continued breaking up to make up. I never let him move back in with me though.

Meanwhile, Willie and I found a friendship that was comfortable. Usually, I called him for advice or to whine and complain about whoever I was dating at the time. If I didn't have a man, I would hang out with Willie until we would break up because I wanted more from him than he was ready to give. One of our obstacles was children. Willie was worried that I would change my mind about wanting children. He had been married and raised two children, and he didn't want me to miss out on motherhood if I decided that I wanted children down the road.

Another thing that happened was that we found out we were both musicians. Willie was more professional than I was, but this would prove to be a special bond later on. Ironically, the company we worked for wanted to make up a band from their employees to perform at a Christmas party. We were shocked to see each other at the meeting. He didn't know I was a singer, and I didn't know he played keyboard.

Born Again

On Martin Luther King Day, in 1993, I had taken the day off work from work. I was browsing the shoe department in Macy's when a woman approached me. She asked if I wanted to go to church with her the following Sunday. To my surprise, I said yes. Even though she was a stranger, I didn't worry because I had been searching for a spiritual outlet.

My first visit to that church was amazing. Everyone was friendly and they all seemed interested in me. I got all charged up about studying the Bible and spending time with nice people. I went through the study program which, among other things, meant forgiving people with whom I had been angry with for years. I called the person who raped me when I was eight years old, and told him that I forgave him. He thanked me in a voice that sounded truly grateful for the forgiveness. When I saw him months later, he treated me like a long lost friend who he was happy to see. He introduced me to his wife and let me hold his babies.

The next person I needed to forgive was Frances, the woman who adopted me. I hated her so much that I was happy when she died. Forgiving her was a struggle, however, it was explained to me that she was suffering in Hell so my hatred was only hurting me, and so I was able to forgive her. I had stopped speaking to her husband (the man), but I made the call to let him know that I forgave him as well. I also tried to reach out and build a father-daughter relationship with him. It never happened. He's now remarried and I have resolved to let him live his life without me.

I continued to ask people who I had wronged in some way for forgiveness, including all the people who I had been intimate with, as this was premarital sex and biblically classified as a sin. It felt good to let go of the bitterness, anger, and hurt that I had been holding onto for so long. By the time I got baptized on Valentine's Day, I really felt reborn.

In the early stages of my newfound Christianity, I was fine with making the adjustments to my life. Anytime I had trouble, I read the Bible, prayed, and talked it through with a trusted friend.

The first major adjustment was moving out of my own place and in with roommates who were members of the church. I had been on my own for three years at this point, so I was not used to sharing my space. It was difficult and I would end up moving and changing roommates three different times within the two and a half years that I stayed in the church.

There also were the lifestyle changes in general but none of these were new to me because of my upbringing. The difference, in this case, was that this was an all encompassing lifestyle that I was choosing, and I was not just following the rules of the house. But, I was happy, too, to learn that I could still wear pants, makeup and listen to whatever type of music I wanted as long as it wasn't obscene or profane. And, I changed the way I dressed. I went from wearing provocative clothes to conservative attire. Plus, I changed the way I talked. I stopped swearing and found other ways to express myself.

My interactions with men drastically changed, too. I only dated men who were members of my church. So, going out on dates was more friends hanging out and having fun. A typical date was when one couple made plans and invited another couple to come along. The planners would then choose the people they wanted to be a part of the date. This was easy-going and comfortable because the church always had plenty of events that were fun to attend. It was also nice because I knew there would be no awkward moments at the end of the date. There was never anything more than a hug. But, when a man and woman became a couple, the situation changes. Now, the couple took turns planning the date and finding another couple with whom they would double. Some couples kissed at the end of a date, but it was up to each couple to make that decision.

It was interesting, but the only time in my life when I was willing to have children was while I was living that lifestyle. I had decided, at a very young age, that I would not have children because of my own unhappy childhood. Because I didn't have perfect vision and I would never be able to keep a child safe. I felt that I would be an awful mother, besides, what man would stick around to help me raise a child?

About a year after I got baptized, a new brother in the church showed up. He was new to California. I started talking to Jack at church and at different functions and he had a great sense of humor. One day Jack's roommate dropped a little hint, asking how I felt about Jack. The roommate let me know that Jack was interested in pursuing a relationship with me. At the time, I was not feeling anything more than friendship. So,

I prayed and asked God to let me know if Jack was the man He wanted me to have in my life. If yes, I wanted Him to let me know.

As time went on, we spent more time together, and I started to like him more and more. Finally, in the summer of 1995, he asked me to be his girlfriend and I agreed. We dated for six months.

One weekend, it was his turn to plan our date. Although I had talked to him at different times during the week, he didn't mention the plan. Earlier in the day I went to a bridal shower, and when I came home, I was not sure if we were going out later that night. During this time, I had moved several times and had changed roommates, too. I was living in a house with three other women, and we had an extra guest staying with us temporarily. So there was always a great deal of hustle and bustle in a house with five women who were getting ready for dates and social events at the church on a Saturday.

The memory of how things unfolded that day is very clear in my mind. I picked up the phone to check for my messages, and our house guest asked what I was doing. I told her and she said "ok." She stood there while I checked and since there were no messages, I just hung up the phone. Later I found out that she was told to make sure that I didn't call Jack's house before my roommate (and spiritual mentor) came home. Ten minutes later my roommate arrived and took me for a ride to the park down the street from our house and asked me when I had last talked to Jack.

"Yesterday."

"How did he sound?"

"Fine, but he never did give me date details."

"Are you sure he sounded normal?"

"Yes I'm sure. Why are you making this a big deal?"

I will never forget what happened next. She took off her sunglasses and looked at me from the driver's seat and told me, "Jack packed up last night, took a bus, and moved back home. He left his roommates a note."

First I argued with her. "No he did not. We have a date today. I just talked to him yesterday."

I went on like that, calling her all kinds of liars, telling her that she had to be joking, and that she could not possibly be telling the truth.

She didn't say another word.

All of a sudden, a giant, invisible hand came from out of nowhere and tried to physically remove my guts and my heart from my body. The pain took my breath away. I screamed, writhed, and begged for it to stop hurting. My grief, this invisible hand, is what pain feels like to me. I physically feel as if a giant hand is trying to remove my insides.

That was the beginning of the end for me and God. I had asked God if Jack was the man He wanted for me and I thought He said yes, Jack was the man. Here I was doing everything I was supposed to do. I had given Jack my heart NOT my body. I gave up so much of my life in order to live like a true Christian. I did what the church leadership said to do. I THOUGHT GOD LOVED ME!

I left the church and moved into my own place, I stopped praying, and my Bible, along with any other books about faith, went into a box in the back of the closet and that's where they stayed for years.

I was able to talk to Jack a few months after he left. I told him the way in which he left was "jacked-up." I called him every name in the book, and I invented some that were not in the book. I didn't hear from him again.

Overall, I will never regret the time I spent living a part of that lifestyle. It definitely was a life-changing experience. I felt loved, and I really wanted to live right. This was the time when I had really found the other side of misery. When I left the church, I left God, and I'm still trying to find my way back to Him.

PART THREE
1995-2006

Getting Myself Together

After leaving the church, I really went wild. I started partying almost every night. I did drugs and drank more than I had ever before and I always had to be around people. It was hard to be at home alone because I had gotten so used to having roommates and the church always had some kind of function going on.

This became a very dark time in my life. I remember walking around waiting for a bus or a truck to be going fast enough so that I could jump in front of it and be killed instantly. They never seemed to be going fast enough. Anytime I heard about people getting hit by the train I would think about it, but I could never find the nerve.

So, I turned to the one thing that I knew would make me feel good. A man. I got involved with one man who was a bigger drama queen than I was.

I had gone on a trip to Las Vegas with my family and I brought home a cherry pie. The day I baked it, I told him that it looked too good to eat even though it had come all the way from Las Vegas. While it cooled off, I left to run an errand, and when I came home he said he had something important to tell me and I should sit down. He knelt down in front of me and took both of my hands in his and looked me in the eyes. "I had a piece of your cherry pie," he said. Since he was being so dramatic about it I decided to be just as dramatic. I snatched my hands away from him and jumped up. I paced around the room with one hand on my hip and pointing the finger of my other hand. "You did what!" I yelled. "How could you do that? I brought that pie all the way from Vegas! I can't believe you had a piece of my pie while I was not here and I haven't even had a piece yet! I wanted to be the one to cut the first piece!"

I yelled and paced around having a fit about the cherry pie. I decided I didn't have enough energy to compete with him in the drama department. I sent him on his way with a piece of cherry pie.

The next guy I hooked up with was violent and prone to throwing things and punching holes in the walls. We didn't get too serious because I was seeing other guys and I just knew he was seeing other women. We were together for one month.

I joined a gospel singing group and that's where I met a musician who I really liked and we got along very well. I was no longer working, as I was enrolled in college, but I had a few months before classes started, so I was home all day doing nothing. We spent all of our time together and we got along well. He made me feel that I was the most important thing in his life. However, once classes started, we began to have problems. He worked a security job and got off late at night and so came over after work. He got upset when I told him we would have to make changes because I needed time to do homework and rest.

From there he started accusing me of being with other men. We had issues with the people in the gospel group. We argued over the way I cooked and what I wore and any other thing that he could find to fuss about.

Things got increasingly difficult, but I stayed with him for about two years. I felt that all the attention he gave me was rare, and I would never find a man who would make me the center of his world.

One day I came home from my friend's wedding to find his stuff gone and a message on my voicemail. I spent months crying myself to sleep.

I finally got so sick of being miserable that I called him and asked him what was so wrong with me? How did I go from being the center of his world to being tossed away like yesterday's trash? He told me that he knew that I was a good woman. He may have said things after that but I don't remember. What I do remember is feeling relieved that some other woman had to deal with him.

During this relationship my rent went up, so I needed to go back to work. I dropped out of college and started attending a vocational school in San Francisco. Once I finished vocational school, I got a job in Foster City, and for the first month, I came home from work on Friday and put on my pajamas and stayed in the house until Monday morning. A few times I tried to go out but I got to the door and changed my mind. I just <u>knew</u> that I would see him out with some other woman.

Willie was a part of my life during those years, so he got to see me before, during, and after the changes I went through. He was also the one man who all other men got compared to and the person I called the most to talk to when these relationships were in turmoil. Sometimes, however, his shoulder was not always available because he was dealing with his own relationships.

But, he helped me get into the first club band. Up until then, I had only done gospel performing, so being in clubs and on stage was very new. I was a nervous wreck for my first few shows. I stayed with that band about six years.

"I'm Thirty"

Since my birthday was so close to New Year's Day, I decided to have my thirtieth birthday party later in the month. But, I had moved so many times that I put the wrong address on the invitations. As a result, I had to stand outside, in the rain, with balloons so that party guests looking for the address would spot me. This was the first time I had ever planned my own party. While I was living at home, I shared a party with two of my nephews who had birthdays at the end of December and mine was in January. The cake always had three names. I was usually the only girl at the parties because my nephews had friends to invite. There were times I got cheated out of two gifts because people would buy me things for Christmas and say Merry Christmas and Happy Birthday.

During the holidays, once I was out on my own, I would wish to be on a cruise ship in the middle of the ocean. I fantasized about leaving right about the time people started getting ready for Thanksgiving and staying on the cruise until after Valentine's Day. On my fantasy cruise there would be no such thing as the holiday season. While Frances was alive our house was the place to be for everyone and I hated every minute of it. I was her kitchen helper and I didn't do anything right, so she spent more time yelling at me, snatching things away from me, or swinging and throwing things at me. Those were also the times when the house was full of people that would grab opportunities to abuse me when there was so much going on that no one missed me.

While I was part of the church, I celebrated my twenty-fourth and twenty—fifth birthdays and they were special. My roommates managed to surprise me both years. So, after I left the church my birthdays were no big deal. But, my thirtieth birthday was different and I was feeling like I wanted to do something special, but I was too full of pride to ask for help. So, some people didn't make it to the party.

Pride would take me on a roller coaster for the next ten years. There were times when pride worked in my favor and times when it worked against me. My party was the first example.

In May of 2000, I changed jobs and started working for a company that was an easier commute. This job was located in downtown San Jose across from a light rail station. That office moved to Mountain View in 2001, which is where my studio apartment was. Now I was close enough to walk to work, and I walked to and from work every day and ate nothing but salads.

During this time, I'd lined up a show for our band at the club where my ex-boyfriend worked. The night we went to do the show, I wore a black second skin patent leather cat suit and strutted my stuff on that stage like I knew I was, "All that and then some." The funny thing is after the show was over and I was getting in the car to go home, I ripped the cat suit right down the middle. Obviously, that was the last appearance the cat suit ever made on stage.

One good thing that happened was that Willie and I became really close when we started doing music together. I moved in with Willie later that year, and I lived with him for two years while I waited for a marriage proposal that never came. When I moved, I did it abruptly and stayed in a motel for a month until I found a place to stay. A woman rented me a room.

Living with this woman was bittersweet. First of all, it was further from work, and since I am nowhere near a morning person, I struggled to get up and out on time. What was sweet is that she got up earlier than me, turned on the heat, and made coffee for me in the morning. It was about a week before I found that the coffee was decaf. She also had a little dog that would sometimes cry in the wee hours of the night, and I have a hard time going back to sleep after being awakened from a deep sleep. On the plus side, I did have my own bathroom and a huge walk in closet. I decorated my room with flower garlands and string lights and called it my Jewel Box. I was the precious jewel that lived in it.

On some mornings she would stand in my bedroom door and clap her hands and sing, "It's time for Kari to get up," over and over until I crawled out of bed. I lived with her a little over a year, but then I wanted my own place.

Even though I was no longer living with Willie, we still dated and we were still in a band together. At my current residence, I was not allowed to have overnight guests and I was not moving back in with Willie without a "ring and a wedding date" (as Dr. Laura would say). She was sad when I moved out, and to make things worse, her dog died one week later. She is a very remarkable woman and I adopted her as one of my moms.

In 2004, the real estate market was booming. I decided to buy a condo in June so I could "pay the cost to be the boss" in my own place.

About a month after I bought the condo, I went to a week-long retreat for people with vision disabilities. It was a time for me to relax and think about what I wanted for my life. At this retreat, I met a man who got me excited about living a life of gratitude and doing what it takes to reach my full potential. His name was Percy Jones.

I met Percy when I was on my way into the camp's nurse's office. I was crying because there was a lady there who was always yelling at and mistreating her guide dog. On this particular day, I got into an altercation with her and I ran to the nurse's office in tears. When I came out, Percy asked what was wrong, and I sat and talked to him for a long time. Over the course of that week, I found out that Percy was a bus driver before he was diagnosed with diabetes. He was in a wheelchair because his legs were amputated below the knees. He had a new heart and new kidneys, and he was completely blind. Moreover, in addition to being in school at the time studying for his Ph.D. in Psychology, he also led a grief counseling group at his church.

We remained close after leaving camp. Though Willie and I were not together, we still talked and we were trying to work things out. Percy lent me his ear "to bend" as I tried to work through the changes. During one of our marathon phone calls, Percy told me that he met a wonderful woman who he was dating. He wanted me to meet her.

One day she was at his house and he put her on the phone with me, and we hit it off right away. Her name was Candy.

As their relationship grew, I became close to them both. I went over and spent time with them, and Candy came and spent a day with me at my condo. Candy was legally blind like me and she was a massage therapist.

Sadly, Percy couldn't come because mine was an upstairs unit with no elevator. One other person who became a vital part of my life was also a friend of Percy's. Joyce had been at the camp that year as well, and I had met her once. Due to her friendship with Percy and the fact that she was also a massage therapist, Candy spent a lot of time with her as well. n 2005, when it was time to go to camp again, Candy, Joyce and I were roommates. Candy and Percy were engaged. We had a blast that week. I got my first chance to see how unshakable Candy was.

One morning at breakfast Percy was being grouchy and bossy. Candy didn't tell him off. She served him with a smile and kept being her sweet self. She went through the week without missing a beat.

The last day of camp was close to the Fourth of July, and Joyce invited us to her house to hang out. Willie and I showed up and hung out for a while. We left kind of early because we had dinner plans. He took me to a romantic restaurant with a piano player and we had a fine dinner and dessert.

I thought we were about to leave when he pulled out a ring and asked me to marry him. On July 2, 2005, Willie and I became engaged. On our way home, he told me to call Percy because he, Candy, and Joyce were waiting to hear the news. I was so excited. Now both Candy and I were engaged. So Candy and I shared wedding planning details, then I was on my own. Candy and Percy were married in September of 2005.

PART FOUR
2006-2011

Lasting Impressions

In 2006 when applications for Enchanted Hills were mailed, mine went unopened. I was not going because I was in wedding planning mode. I was also working and saving my vacation days for the wedding and honeymoon. I called everyone and told them to have a great time.

A week after camp was over I called to see how it went and if everyone had enjoyed another good time. I was told that Percy had passed away. He went into the hospital the day before they were to leave and was released after a short stay. He died a few days after his release.

When I called, Candy answered the phone and gave me the news as if she was telling me about someone she had read about in the paper. I was the one having the fit. She never lost her composure. Candy went through a lot of changes with the wedding and the move and now her husband was dead before they even celebrated their one year anniversary. Funerals can bring out ugliness in people, but Candy was the picture of poise and grace throughout the entire ordeal. I remember thinking that I hope I can be that strong. I was inconsolable at Percy's funeral. I could not accept the reality that Percy wouldn't be at our wedding. Willie is twenty years my senior and I know that he may go before me.

I learned later that Joyce and Candy missed our ceremony and had to leave the reception early due to a lack of convenient public transportation. As I think about it now, it was probably better for Candy that way. I can't imagine what she would have felt like sitting through my wedding after having had her own wedding just a year before and losing her husband a mere nine months later. My one regret is that I never gave her a copy of the video of the wedding day. At least then she could have watched it whenever she felt ready.

My Perfect Day

For my wedding, I wanted a place with a water feature, but I also had to take into consideration that some people might not be able to deal with stairs. I also didn't want to run around on my wedding day. I wanted a place that could accommodate the ceremony and reception. So, when I saw the Freedom Hall and Gardens, I fell in love with the location and made all my plans with that place in mind.

My three bridesmaids were as different temperament-wise as size-wise, so I told the ladies in no uncertain terms that they were responsible for finding their own dresses. I didn't want to be responsible for making them wear some ugly dress that would end up in a donation bag.

There was other "ugliness" for me to handle in preparing for our day. Here I am 36 years old and finally planning my wedding. One thing I was not having was Mr. H (Frances' husband) walking me down the aisle and giving me away. Mr. H's wife was taking liberties with who to invite from her family but offered no financial help. Because of further bickering, I sent both of them a letter letting them know that I didn't want them to attend my wedding. A round of phone calls from Mr. H's wife and a multitude of emails from her youngest daughter didn't dissuade me from my original decision.

A week before the wedding, a friend of Mr. H's wife went to see her and brought me back a beautiful silk flower arrangement in a ceramic basket. There was also a ceramic bride and groom that stands about a foot tall and two ceramic butterflies all in my wedding colors of different shades of purple.

The weather was on our side as the wedding was held outside and, although folks found shade to sit in instead of the bride and groom's seating we'd arranged, my brother's oldest son Tyler, walked me down the aisle. Also all of the processional music was instrumental because I didn't want a singer taking away attention from whomever was being escorted down the aisle, namely me. My cousin, Vicky, and her husband stood in as my parents that day and they came along with Willie's parents to light the unity candle that symbolized the two families joining.

I had written a passage about what the day symbolized. Someone from the bridal party said "jump the broom not the groom," and I replied, "I'll jump the groom later." Next, the best man (Willie's brother) pretended to lose the ring and patted his pockets. Ironically, my ring was missing a diamond and Willie lost his ring while we were packing for our honeymoon. He later found it in the suitcase while on our honeymoon.

The ceremony ended as we finished our vows (written by us), jumped the broom, and danced down the aisle to "This Will Be" by Natalie Cole. Our ceremony was quick because I wanted to get on with the party.

The reception was the best part of the day. We had a couple do two dance performances and one of our band members sang a song to us, and I sang "At Last," but since I didn't know the words, my wedding coordinator stood behind me and told me the words. Willie was handcuffed and had to take my garter off with his teeth, and he danced like James Brown to "I Feel Good," with the garter in his mouth and the handcuffs on until his brother got them off.

A good time was had by all and we even had the photographer follow us home to get a picture of Willie carrying me over the threshold. We took our last picture and collapsed onto our bed still in our wedding clothes.

Honeymoon Blues

We were scheduled to leave for our honeymoon on Monday 9/25 at 9 p.m. The Town Car picked us up and drove us to San Francisco airport. We waited in line but when it was our turn to get our tickets and check our luggage, we had a problem. This was 2006, before one needed a passport to travel out of the county and a birth certificate would work. The problem was that all Willie had was a photocopy of his birth certificate. We were going to Mexico and the agent was not going to give him a ticket. I was so tempted to leave without him. We did get a voucher for a hotel close by, stayed overnight, and got up early the next day. I called the travel agent who booked the trip and told her what happened. She changed our dates so we could leave Tuesday night. I then told Willie to leave and if he didn't return with a document that would allow him to travel, he better not come back. It took a few hours and a lecture from the immigration officer, but he got a passport and we left for Mexico that night.

The flight was awful. I, for one, hate to fly. And, because I was trying to save money, I bought cheap tickets. What I didn't realize was that we ended up taking one plane from San Francisco to Chicago and another plane from Chicago to Mexico. Then, we got off the plane in Mexico we were looking for the booth of the company that would take us to the resort. Instead we ended up paying for a timeshare presentation and listening to a sales pitch. Then we missed our shuttle and had to wait an hour.

The shuttle ride was so long that by the time we got to the resort all we wanted was sleep, which didn't come easy. The resort operators informed us that the time-share presentation we signed up for was a scam, and they would refund our money if we agreed to see their presentation instead. Of course we agreed because we wanted our money.

When we finally got into our room, it was wonderful. It had a large bed with lots of pillows, a Jacuzzi tub for two, and every day the staff would fold the towels on the edge of it in different shapes like birds and flowers. The room also had a mini-fridge that stayed stocked with drinks. These were great to mix with one of four spirits that one could enjoy by placing a glass under a nozzle and pressing a lever and a shot would pour into it. There was tequila, rum, brandy, and scotch. We tried to mix all four of them to see what would happen. What happened was we got a headache and slept a day away.

Since Vodka was my favorite, I spent more time at the swim up bar. The room had a private patio with a two-person hammock which Willie and I tried out the first night and I fell out of.

The resort had round the clock food and drinks that we could order from room service or go to one of four restaurants: Italian, Japanese, Mediterranean and a steakhouse. We tried all but the Mediterranean. When we ate at the Japanese place, the waiter challenged us to see which one of us would finish a cup of sake first. Of course, I won. What I won was another cup of sake. I liked this restaurant the best because it was funny to see Mexicans dressed like samurais.

We only ventured off of the resort a few times. One day we went to see Mayan ruins and another day we went to a resort that was just opening after repairs from storm damage. On the last day we went on a dinner cruise. We walked a Zen garden and went to the beach. We went to shows and events at the hotel. One was a magic show, and I got to be the magician's assistant. Another show was a contest where four men got picked from the crowd (Willie was one), and they had to copy all of these movements in sequential order and not make a mistake. Willie won a bottle of tequila, which never saw California. We spent seven days there and by day five, I was ready to come home.

A Model of Inner Peace

As I was spending my first Christmas as Mrs. Kelley, Candy was waiting for some important test results. The tragic results came before the New Year. She had stage four breast cancer. Again, as she told me this news, she sounded like she was talking about some distant relative who she'd heard about. She was very matter-of-fact as she took me through the "to do" list while I had a breakdown. I never saw her down or discouraged. We spent time together when we could, and she was always busy being grateful for still being alive.

What started my journey

I quit my job in March of 2007. This was neither wise nor was it planned. I still had my condo and I didn't have another job lined up yet. I left the job on such bad terms that I had to fight for unemployment. Needless to say, I didn't get any references from that job in spite of working there for almost seven years.

I submitted my resume and completed the interviewing process. Due to the previous job in Foster City, I had all of the adaptive equipment that I needed to do the work that the job required. There were agencies in place to help people with disabilities be successful at work. It was the agency's job to make sure that my adaptive equipment was compatible with the equipment that the company used. This is how I began my lesson about the value of perseverance.

The best way to describe what I went through would be to compare it to the "Who's on first? What's on second?" the comedy routine performed by Abbot and Costello.

I got the run around for a while so I didn't talk to anyone who could not make things happen for me. One piece of advice that I remembered getting from a woman that I adopted as a mom was, "Your stuff is not important to anyone but you."

I also told him that anyone who took the time and spent the money to get a Master's degree wouldn't last six months. Shortly after that, I had an altercation with my coworker about her whispering sessions, and I stopped speaking to her. From then on, if it was not work related, we did not talk. This made the area very difficult for our department since my cubicle was in the middle of the three in that area. I didn't care. I was mean to her. She had significant medical concerns at the time, and I couldn't have cared less if she dropped dead on the spot.

I was planning my wedding at the time so I made sure everyone else got invited to the wedding shower and the wedding except her. I didn't try to fix that relationship until a couple of weeks before I got married.

After I got married, Willie got an earful every day about how unhappy I was. He later told me that he dreaded asking me about my day because he knew it would turn into a long, loud dissertation.

I became very disgusted and felt unsupported with overall management, especially by my manager. I realized that he felt he had permission to express unprofessional information and opinions.

Two incidents that support this fact come to mind. The first one was after I was married, and I was wearing some jewelry that Willie had given me. My manager commented on it and I said that jewelry is the way to a girl's heart.

"That's not what my wife's into," he said.

When I asked what she was into and he replied, "bondage," I told him that was too much information.

The second incident took place at February's staff meeting. We were discussing a caller who referred to herself as "queer." I said that it was interesting that someone would use that term when he said, "Kari, you and your friends refer to each other as 'nigger' sometimes, don't you?"

I let him know that my friends and I didn't engage in such foolishness.

About a month after that incident, we had a run in. He was requiring me to do something that I felt would be a problem with my vision disability. I felt he was setting me up for failure, and I told him he was an ass. I used a few four letter words to express what I thought of him and his style of management. Then I walked off the job. I didn't have the inner strength to be unaffected by the treatment I received.

Once I left my job, I knew I would have to go back to school. While I was working, I got the idea in my head that I wanted to be a life coach. I presented myself to the government agency that would assist me and the struggle began. Even though I found a school that met the criteria, it was suggested that going to college was a better idea and it would be easier to get approval. I enrolled in September 2007, and I did very well for the first quarter.

The spring semester began in January 2008, and I made the mistake of taking a Math class. Beginning Algebra was a nightmare. I was taking this class for the second time. To make matters worse, I needed specialized equipment in order to see what the instructor was doing. This equipment didn't arrive until the middle of the quarter, so I dropped all of my classes. It would take me four tries to get a C in Beginning Algebra.

I took classes during the summer and tried to tackle Intermediate Algebra in September 2008. Not only did I flunk Algebra, but because I was so focused on Math that I flunked the other two classes I was taking as well.

This sent me to bed and I could not stop crying for weeks. I had to increase my antidepressants and even add one more. I kept trying college until I realized that I was not going to reach my original goal as a life coach, and financially, I needed to get back to work. I found what I thought was a solution and presented it to the agency.

I heard about a program in Arkansas that was specially designed for people with vision disabilities to train in different professions and be placed in a job. I convinced myself that I had to do this because I could neither put my resume out and get hired, nor could I continue in college. As much as I wanted to be a life coach, there was no way for me to pay for it on my own. I contacted a friend who had gone through the program and got detailed information about the place, the training, and the job that I would be doing once I finished the training. As I listened to her describe the entire program, I knew I would absolutely hate it. However, I felt that this was the last chance for me to get a job.

I filled out the forms and received my one way ticket to Arkansas. My remaining time was spent celebrating Thanksgiving and Christmas, packing, planning, and celebrating my 40th birthday. The plan was for me to go to Arkansas for six months, come back to California, and begin a job that I would have to stay with for two years before I could transfer. I had battle after battle with people close to me about why I was leaving for so long and how awful things were going to be for me in Arkansas. The one person who supported me was my husband.

I left for Arkansas two weeks after turning 40. The day I left was one of the hardest days I ever had. I held onto Willie for dear life, and I cried for most of the first leg of my flight. During the second leg of the journey, I got a couple of shots of liquid courage also known as Vodka and started one of the many pep talks I would give myself. By the time I got to Arkansas, it was late at night. It was very cold. I met a few people, talked to my new roommate, and settled in for the night.

Things didn't' work out for me in Arkansas. The program requirements were either a college degree or work experience in the financial field in order to qualify. I was not made aware of this until I was almost three weeks into the thirty-day evaluation period. The evaluation period is designed to make sure that a person with a vision disability has the skills to live independently. It was not enough that I had lived on my own for years. Never mind that I had bought and sold a condo on my own. It didn't matter that I had not only planned and paid for my perfect wedding and also handled two major home improvement projects, a complete bathroom remodel and a new roof on our house. So, I spent three weeks showing them that I knew how to make a bed, pack a suitcase, do my own laundry, and cook for myself. I took typing, reading, and Basic Math tests.

Many California tax dollars were sent to Arkansas for this foolishness and I was never qualified to even start the training. The only benefit from this experience is that I learned that I can adapt to a place other than

California if I ever had to. Although I was used to almost constant sunshine, I learned to deal with freezing rain. I made some pretty cool friends as well. However, I returned home feeling like a very angry failure.

I had no idea what I was going to do with my life now that I was back at home. I went through the usual job search steps and met with the California State Department of Rehabilitation counselor. I started to consider going back to college as much as I knew that it was not really what I wanted. I started thinking about having my own business or singing full time. But, I could not get excited about any of it.

Memorable Moments

Candy was out of town for my fortieth birthday party, but we talked on the phone when she got back. The evening we talked just happened to be the same day she got the news that she had about one year to live. I can't imagine even answering the phone after getting this kind of news. I broke down while she remained calm and composed.

In late February, I was on the phone with Candy and she talked about wanting to go to Sedona, Arizona before she got too sick to travel. I said I would like to go just to spend time with her. Willie encouraged me to go in spite of the fact that it would put a strain on our finances. He pointed out that the time spent with a good friend was much more valuable than staying home worrying about money. We made the arrangements, and Candy, Joyce and I took off for seven days.

Three Blind Mice and a Dog

Little did I know that this trip to Arizona would be the beginning of a healing process for me. Sedona is well known for energy vortexes and it has a large number of sacred places established by Native Americans. It was our goal to visit these places as well as indulge in spa treatments and spiritual readings. Joyce was able to set us up with our own personal tour guide who was also a Shaman. The hotel where we stayed had a driving service that we could use to go places on our own as well. The staff, at our hotel, became very impressed with our independence and named us the, Three Blind Mice. One staff member was a very good photographer and took pictures of some beautiful sunsets and sent them to us.

Our tour guide took us to some places that were not the usual tourist attractions. One place had a medicine wheel that we were able to walk. Another place was near the water and we sat on boulders and he played his flute for us. I remember feeling very peaceful there. We took a picture and it exemplifies how calm we all were. Even Vivian, Joyce's guide dog, seemed to be somewhere she have could stayed forever. We visited the cathedral on the hill twice, and it was during the second visit that I felt movement in my heart.

On this particular day there was a choir singing and anyone who wanted could light a candle to place at the front. The choir sang a verse over and over until everyone had placed their candle at the front. I don't remember the song, but I remember asking God why I was not feeling any of this wonderful energy, and was I just here seemingly taking up space. I told God how tired and frustrated I was that I was perfectly healthy and Candy was the one who only had limited time. Right there I went into a "pity party" about how I was without any real purpose. I asked God why He didn't just take me instead.

The night before we came home, we each had a session with an energy healer. During my reading, she told me information about my childhood and we talked about Frances, my mother. This healer was able to let me know that she, Frances, wanted me to forgive her and she was sorry. These feelings and deep-rooted issues have hindered my life in a big way and I'm still working on forgiving.

Joyce, Candy, and I shared our readings with each other, and I was able to share many stories about my upbringing with them. I also learned a lot about them, and we became even closer. These two women were able to help me on my way to forgiveness.

Accepting My Gifts

Recent events in my life have given me a deep desire to search for the inner peace that sustains you when you are experiencing hard times.

On September 11th of 2010, my pillar of strength was gone, Candy passed away. Even as she knew her days were numbered, she was busy keeping everyone else inspired and she never lost her joy for life. The last time I was with Candy, we had a long talk. When it was time for me to leave, she hugged me and rubbed my back. We had once named her Lady Tranquility, and so she said she was rubbing her tranquil energy off on me.

On January 16th 2011, I received a call that my brother was not expected to live through the week. I went to see him in the hospital and even though he slept through my visit, I said my goodbye. He passed away on January 20th. My brother was one of my few family members that I was able to count on. Even though his children were the same age as me, he made me feel like I was his little sister. Wherever he took them, I went too. I got a nickname just like they did and he always stayed in touch when I got busy trying to be grown up.

During my life I have experienced unspeakable pain. I have sat in judgment of people who carried on so dramatically when they lost a loved one. What I have now learned is that the loss of a loved one is devastating, especially when this is one person who showed you unconditional love when most others around you showed otherwise. Having the realization that the one face that lit up when it saw you is gone forever is beyond words. Knowing the arms that wrapped around you will never touch you again and the unmistakable voice that said, "I love you" is forever silent is almost too much to bear. No matter what others might say in an effort to comfort you, there is no comfort in knowing that the person is in a better place while you have to live without that incredible someone.

The search is on

An invisible hand showed up and knocked me to the floor. A couple of weeks later, I woke up in one of those moods where I was determined to get a lot done. I put on some music and began to clean the house. All of a sudden, I found myself on the couch howling and moaning from the pain. I got back in bed and stayed there for the rest of that day.

Nowadays, I pray for the ability to forgive myself as well as others because I want things to be right when it's my turn to leave this life. I am trying to come to terms with my past. I feel that I'm entitled to know exactly what happened when I was a year old to cause the optic nerve damage. In my effort to find this information, I deal with the frustration and runaround of bureaucracy. I sign up on websites and send e-mails to talk show hosts and TV personalities that say they can help me. I have paid fee upon fee and nothing comes back but form letters and automated response e-mails. I will not give up.

I am in the process of developing my relationship with God. In the book written by Julie Cameron; *The Right to Write: An Invitation and Initiation Into the Writing Life*; she gave God the title of Good Orderly Director. When I think of God as the Ultimate Director of my life I am free to give Him the reverence and honor that He deserves.

I think of my life as the blockbuster movie that God is directing. I find myself excitedly looking forward to see what the next scene has in store for me and who will be the cast and crew. I absolutely love the leading man God chose for me. Our running joke now is that I was his midlife crisis and he's still having it. Although it took 16 years for us to get married, I'm so glad we didn't get married sooner. The years between our first date and our wedding served to help me appreciate what a wonderful man Willie is. We had to break up and make up for those years and I learned valuable lessons that I may not have learned otherwise.

I love that He strategically put people in my life in certain roles to counter-balance the negative messages with messages of encouragement and love such as the instructor who paid my tuition at the private school I attended from sixth through eighth grades. And, this instructor was also instrumental in getting me into high school.

During that time people who lived in my area were bussed to a different school, so I had not been in touch after I graduated from high school. But, I tracked him down and met he and his wife for dinner to personally thank them. Yes, it took me five years to graduate from high school because I was busy screwing up. At the time I didn't understand why he was so hurt when he found out I wasn't graduating on time. He did show up the next year to say better late than not at all. I invited him and his wife to my wedding, and they won the grand prize for being married the longest. The prize was a bottle of champagne and the chance to advise the newlyweds on the secret for staying married. Their advice was, "be careful."

Today I truly believe that I am blessed to be alive. I believe that everything I have experienced has helped me to appreciate where I am today. There were many times I woke up disappointed that I was still alive. I spent years trying to figure out how to end my life. If I had all the money that I have spent on counseling, psychiatrists, antidepressant drugs, and self help programs, I would be a multimillionaire. Only divine intervention kept me from getting pregnant or turning to prostitution. The fact that I never became addicted to any of the myriad recreational drugs that I tried is truly miraculous.

I am enormously grateful for my life today. My life experience allows me to relate to a host of people who may need a listening ear and a compassionate heart to help them when they get stuck in the places where I got stuck. I realize that throughout my life I will still get stuck and God will provide me with what I need to get unstuck. I have now chosen to believe that every experience that I have is in perfect synchronicity with the grand plan of my life's purpose. A very valuable lesson that I have learned is that I do have unconditional love right now.

On January 30th I came to be writhing and begging for mercy but not because of pain. Just like the heart and body can feel unspeakable pain, they can also feel unspeakable pleasure. I still have a face that lights up when it sees me. I still have a strong pair of arms that wrap around me and

I still have a voice that says it loves me. On this day I also received some information that will help me find my birth family and get the answers I am looking for.

In the meantime I will live every moment in gratitude and appreciation. I will continue to come to terms with the challenges that come my way and seek the lessons to be learned in each one of them.

On May 9th 2011 I was told a story about my birth mother. According to this information she was a young woman on the verge of being a star when she got pregnant with me and her rise to stardom ended. She gave me a severe beating that caused optic nerve damage. I had an emotional melt down. I couldn't understand why she didn't just terminate the pregnancy.

As I processed the information I got angry and decided that I wanted to find my birth mother and show her what my life turned out to be. I wanted to let her see just how independent I am and what a beautiful life I have in spite of not having perfect eyesight. So in June 2011 I started a focused and determined search for my birth story. It took an entire year to find the information. My birth story, when it finally came, was not even close to what I was told. None of the stories that I had been told over the years of how I lost my eyesight turned out to be true.

My birth mother was thirty six years old, married to a military man. They had two daughters. While my birth mothers husband was overseas she was raped at gunpoint. Her rapist was arrested for murder. When she realized she was pregnant she and her husband decided to give me up for adoption. My birth mother didn't even give me a first name. She felt that was for my new family to do.

I was placed in fostercare immediately and was loved and well taken care of. When I was nine months old I was adopted by a family consisting of a mom, dad and a five year old sibling. It is in this home that I am abused by the mother. I am beaten and shaken. While she is shaking me she bumps my head. For a week and a half I am sluggish and sleepy. During that week and a half fluid is collecting around my brain. The fact that I'm alive at all is miraculous.